"These poems aren't meant to "be sung/ on arrival" for they just keep on arriving in prodigious arcs always delightful and unexpected, where every word persuades us to keep following on, furiously trying to keep up."

—D.S. Marriott

ALSO BY EMILY CRITCHLEY

When I say I Believe Women... (London: bad press, 2006)
Of All the Surprises (Switzerland: Dusie, 2007)
Who handles one over the Backlash
        (Old Hunstanton, Norfolk: Oystercatcher Press, 2008)
Hopeful For Love Are Th' Impoverish'd Of Faith
        (Southampton: Torque Press, 2010)
Love / All That / & OK: Selected Writing
        (London: Penned in the Margins, 2011)
Sonnets for Luke (Liverpool: Holdfire press, 2011)
IMAGINARYLOVEPOEMS (Paris: Corrupt Press, 2011)
This is not a True Thing (London: Intercapillary Press, 2013)
Some Curious Thing (London: Barque Press, 2016)
Ten Thousand Things (Norwich: Boiler House Press, 2017)

EMILY CRITCHLEY

Arrangements

Shearsman Books

First published in the United Kingdom in 2018 by
Shearsman Books
50 Westons Hill Drive
Emersons Green
BRISTOL
BS16 7DF

www.shearsman.com

Shearsman Books Ltd Registered Office
30–31 St. James Place, Mangotsfield, Bristol BS16 9JB
(this address not for correspondence)

ISBN 978-1-84861-604-2

ACKNOWLEDGEMENTS
Poems from *Arrangements* have appeared in *PN Review,*
Cordite Poetry Review, Chicago Review and *Granta.*

Contents

With thanks to Kelvin Corcoran and Tony Frazer
for their advice and support.

And for Alex Goodall without whom.

Arrangements

In the middle of the journey of our life…

Dante Alighieri, *La Divina Commedia*

this

is the abstract, this
is the cold doing, this
is the almost impossible

Charles Olson, 'In Cold Hell, in Thicket'

Then you thought me up

But for nothing, which is some poetry,
we would not have
metrically speaking
some kind of root cause or connecting
detail.

The bus – which doesn't have wings
or settle in Greenwich –

because of that park, that sky,
where we each have trod probably
even the same space at the same time only
mythologizing.

Come near
I'm your queen.
Even if you can't
reason wildly
I'm all for those places
I don't think we will ever not go to
or recognize.

There are too many senses
– lexically speaking –
too many meaning-shoots. Then there's the way you breeze
filmically onto a Poem Scene.

I don't think, but it does not matter
because when an idea
          is set to spin on its side so
                         you can still be in exile
commuting cherry blossom –

          now I know
I'm the highest bidder
          am literally,
                    wasn't meant to be sung
          on arrival.

          Now that the clouds are pink & an image is wrong as
          something as what is,
you can have it, transactional sense; I exchange for a bark,
                    a touch of my cold feet,
suspended belief.

                    What else can you have
is just that knowledge, just as it is.
                    I will share wth yr body of knowledge
                              that glows on the water, coming past
          Greenwich,   closed body of knowledge.

          This is how to respond when –
                    but this is how to negotiate
          once you begin
                    in a future moon

which – but I can't be moved

any more,

not even your prosody bores me.

I'm lunatic, counting the tide ripples, adding them

up so to see how time made it

so far yet we still

and are not quite ready to meet.

An optical device that led to photography. The device consists of a box
or room with a hole in one side

By tracery   fix
-ings shall we call it or
                    fizzings by all hell
          or atoms or / smaller than that / and
                    colder /
by quarks once you start getting down to it.
          Supra-nucleic
do we grow from love. But we do not grow
     from light, only love
so nastic.

               God that we could raise ourselves up
                    out of the cold blueness of judgement,
          be nearly ourselves in
                    view of developing reason.

               God that like paper, wedded to marks,
                    scrutinized tracings, raw as in
instruments, thorns
          in the desert, doomed trumpet calls
would she find herself
          but obscured only momently. Or what must he do
                    to be perfectly
          not to blame
                    in each moment?

Does he raise it & lower with each new game
or razing the ground that she
doesn't stand
for.

More clicking required perhaps, more light
and more
day.

In world bright as hell
– in not *camera obscura.*   Our youth
was that superabundance of stasis.

And they are over it. Years
without pride, and / or privilege,
not even call or / and song.

She has worked for that clearing. Knows her way round a space
more incisive than thicket.

Not the forbidden,
just not the cold shine of exterior lying
in morning.

For she is no goddess! No, nor
dog neither.

How shall she turn
one to the other, how

accept a reversal

from he

who has shunned the real

(pinholes for distance)?

How accept blood

that he draws without

thinking afterward.

The brush it is clearing, cold is it moving

through that.

Silver as veins of a moon's

eye view.

Not daring to move a muscle. Not daring neither

to try nor to lose. Picking apart one

by each other.

Fear in an uncertainty principle.

+ we must talk quickly + very quiet

Ah annexed is the day's waste
and time it vanishes like whenever
there is nothing worth happening going on
i.e. no schedule for tomorrow's move forward towards death
• the periodization of money
• the historical nature of lust.

Ay, and next to you, love is very last
but permanent
          / displaced? Precisely said, yes.
Yrs is worth the silence of too much said.
Yrs is eagerly believable;
nothing but evidence could possibly break
                              through it.

And there were stars
but none of them were out
          / predictable.

In yr dream you did divine water
– did you divide water –
with as much success.
I've had enough water to be dreamt,
no matter what else is said or not said.

And we can have no more to do
with one another's ontologies
of meaning being 'specially not
loving. Or economic mutilation
or adverse wonder. Only live
by what each other once meant
on other subjects;

       larger than imaginings,

       longer as each day goes on. The real condition is:
no development and definitely,
no, not any kind of containment.

I remember the hounds:

Bells a-jangling
round their throats,
feasting on nostalgia
-carcasses & dumb
luck. Their job
is to come salivate
whenever you
approach. Then it is
to tear that limb
from limb
apart. Lastly
O they lick
the very nerves
they cause. Beautiful
soft fur / rapacious
eyes. Cocking
their leg poolside
for another cur. Or
if in the small
distance you can't hear
me calling
– down boy! –
that's your fucking
problem.

for D.S. Marriott

Sheer fertility of the green grass being over there, while I am here, & which, structured perfectly beneath the feet, to take breath, everyone's, away from them, held out till springy, more perfect, each step that I take it from it or makes the day feel longer, being the answer to the perfect agony of life. Hopping first this way then that until shortness of day met by shortness of breath. Bound by my heavy feet which dragging, no springing to touch & thought I'd made softer touch to the grass, made arrangements with greenness, not marred in that sunny, insensitive newness. But no one can really stay green for that long when it comes it comes spreading it under our feet & is everything set up for the end.

No title (Last year at Marienbad)

for Sascha Akhtar

The fur and glue were not enough.

    They were pretty enough. Just not clear enough. Or maybe

too clear. Yes, it was the translucent glue they used. The kind

    preservers of best moments know best

to avoid. It was the opaqueness of the trees

    along the path. It was the déjà vu: the maze of modernist,

lost shadows stuck structurally before a phase. It was

    intensely tender, too tender, little bits of fur

kept coming off. The glue stuck to my hands

    suspiciously like blood, the feet wldnt stay down

beside their own shadows. My hands were literally not mine

    any more, only the coatings of hands.

Little stupid hands.

    It was enough to fill a whole night with the memory

of grief, but not a whole year. Definitely

    not two. And it was sweet: a glimmer, then

a squeak of hope but, finally, snuffed out

    in daylight by a single

double take, remember?

'In the evening / Everything has a schedule'

You're not allowed to die before we've loved all the exhaustion,
all the disappointing places, kissed them like shadows
to sleep. I forbid you from dying. Mountains on your lips,
grass resting in your eyes.

I didn't want this story: lack the amazement. You should never
have offered yourself as a guide. Also, your lover's sweet
and I would no harm come to either of you.

Just as we never come to ideas; they come to us.
Just as we never want in words; they want in us.

You see it now as we truly believe. I am wishing on your side.
Not even the night-time blows about reminding me of disaster.

1.

for Oli Hazzard

I'll do what they suggest, even though the tide
is a particular mess. Still, I think it's true.
And explaining the thought does at least
offer a somewhat pleasant postponement
of a somewhat non-distinct destiny.

2.

Though I was wrong, so I am not wrong.
To tell you the facts, I am explaining somebody
else's feeling. Though foolishly. Thunder in my heart,
a quite electrical disturbance. I think it might be true.
And those thoughts fly overhead like geese getting
used to the moonlight. O – is he here too? *She*
couldn't lie though there was always something untrue.
But – I told you!

3.

for Rachael Allen

Joy sparks the day warm and we see you,

fine rain, perhaps without example,

though indeed blue shadow always resumes

the rest of the year. Who cares?

Anyway. There is no far out secret

looking for the rose-coloured mood.

First, dear one, but everybody

is so busy or loved, I doubt they would

parade for love. I see there is an

uniform, and talk. And we must catch a view

– the faded pink one. Slowly we

look! The patio, the music. What more

is there to know before the piano,

we don't care!

Revelation in disguise

for Amy Cutler and Sophie Seita

Yes, they are alive and not like triangles,
And I, in my soul, am alive too.
I feel I must shout and write, to tell
Of this in a way, that knowing you may be drawn from me.

And I do amid the noise of casual isolation,
Machinery of history, the chance to sing of us
Superseded by you, is you.
You hold me to the light in a way

I would always have expected, and yet still am surprised, perhaps
Because you always tell me the idea supersedes us, perhaps
You are right. Yet the great spaces loom.
Between our kind. I am ever yours to be forfeited, to desire.

I cannot ever think of me, if I begin
I am back in a room in which the chairs ever
Have their backs toward me,
Pelted by words, actual light

That laugh off suggestion, go on producing Art
Under a general wing, same wild light of the day
That is always true. I pledge me to an idea
I was assigned by birth, which I cannot ever stop remembering.

Remembering to remember. Remember to pass beyond you into the us
In the winged shadow, the space you will never know.
Taking me from myself, the path
Which the blind birth of the day has consigned me to.

I prefer 'us' in the plural, I want 'us'.
You should go from me, all victorious and whole
Like the light and the day.
And then I start getting this feeling of exhaustion.

Opposite of good

Despair breath and it is pointless
that antonym, heliotropic
that control, lost in a minute button!

Or, when I wanted to watch you but you were gone or you wanted
to leave the country – literally cycle to death – even though

Now I am photophobic, you have made me hate the sun,
all growing things, and now I seek the end in small animal bones
or pearls for eyes and then I should have explained –
that reference – what is it you wanted and

It did begin with you
it did begin with you
you thought the most explicit
feelings, even non-directionally

You should have known
you should have known
that's why poems teach us
not to be so obvious.

Or the Shortness of the Day

And so we do, do we, set traps for only us
            then wait for time to shift. Peel each part –
little bits of plaster coming off to view the skin
            beneath it fast becoming not comfortable
in our own or is it knowledge that is changing.
            Skin that wants that feeling when it should not
have. And then the bags of hurt. Never
            were comfortable. Not from the start.
So is the wonder we are still addicted to the pull
            of it at all. Shut off from constant light
or OK, even after memory of pain.
            And yet and yet our holding it against us,
memory of saying in the way of things,
            as if the movement's body didn't catch us both
out, as if that's not the meaning of the originary wound:
            to be held up, flesh word against word,
even as or if those weaknesses were wrongly
            (in that split moment did I not want
uncovered everything about you
            even though as everything I did) always but
I do.

            Permanence is what comes lastly, like
that creeping doubt. The air. No need to shut that up
            all gathered calculations, all vast data, reify
our points after-wrds, add a little to our separate world

view. Right to the point we should dissect that;
change each other's meanings just a little,
        meet each other just a moment
longer, hermeneutically. Not holding one's
        aloneness so rightly till the skin beneath
it cannot breathe

                / or move.

Natura Morta

Where with a light brush, where I mix the wheat
from the lead the thunder
from the threatening, augury
       of fallen birds.

These days lit up by difference alchemize.
Much more than singing a defence.

Listen.
       They could tell
you about
nothing –
biting off one's wings
in spite, bitten, repeated,
       – real blood
circling
the distance.

Afterwards

Go out into the world, and there it is. Do what you can.
At night the line shakes up like memory. The fault Platonic,
not divided or divine. At night look at the women
all exciting (little darlings) they do adorn your dinner
table so. Go out into the world, and there it is

tomorrow facing outwards. Choose your eating place with care,
drag it down the hill (the little darlings will trail after),
make them feel special, at night, the sea changes. Seeds
are split amongst numbers, sex is traded for hurt parchments.
At night there it is: the next day strangled by sunlight.

The big nothing, the twenty somethings before or after –
in day the public confession caught by everyone
against salt against spilling your guts out spiritually,
an easy vindication. At night amongst other
things. The limit or same. But at night it is there.

The cutlery, the condiments we pass round specially.
Whetting our sharp tongues against stone. The boredom. Enough.
But there it always is – preceding you in the door frame,
issuing like moth flames behind. At night the fire's
more enticing. The winelight spitting us out and there it is:

elements of higher things (ambitious little darlings)
– too easily placed – coming through for us. But yesterday
the closed field of music was arch-failure. At night your replies
to mine were swift like ink against the palms of hands,
against the metaphors of body, and we are too often used

and we know this (little darlings) and after us
comes night. Repair your plan. Take what is not yours
more easily. Do it failingly, do it like you
mean to in the night. Not love used as a simile
for this or any other longing, but full of self-regard

– in spite and even because of what is due to night.
Empty the glass before you, leave what's left behind.
Do it lightly and with care, not love, in case of an emotional
                                        foreshadowing:
a crowd of moth dust following you out. At night
you have your memories

around to choose from, forget about the rest,
literally fuck it. The flame can't get you,
not at night; though by the day
you'll languish for a sense of feeling, no, thought. Go out
into the world. Leave everything else.

Movement waving not sleeping

I do not know
There is coral below the surface

Sara Wintz, *Lipstick Traces*

all corners else o' the earth

William Shakespeare, *The Tempest*

the play of those bodies of water

energies of the meeting of different bodies

/ the different water

/ those island

/ mine   (body of water)

in full field
      of leaves

with you over there.

& me here.

/ yours

(same invisible coral /)

            in
movement water

of invisible clashing waters / for so long / invisible bodies
    / for how long between

when we first we made bodies on that island

(make me sleep again)

then swim
        / energies among

where
waving of grass

humming of grass is

total bodies of sea glass dream-swimming

in the
            / movement light
            / cross the
            / wet light / cross the
            clashing of glass the

clear blue energies where we
invisible water

lit up where you
  / coral.

in between / I reach over across &
       reach over across &
       look across / dreaming over
       touch thru the /

earth you have really
    you can always have been

seen
thru me
movement
/ water

where
/ play onto you / like you / play onto me

in the how long waters

& play
thru & thru
& thorough & through

(total energies movement of sea-dream waving not sleeping)

wch waves
/ leaves
thru play
thoro play
through play
thorough play

same bodies energies　　　　/ movement
　　　among

or swim the
     delight & hurt not

& glass is enough / & thorough / & new
     in the

different finding waters

that clear on one side & clouds
        on the other

thoro mine / through looking

thorough your / thru waving

& the through / the sea-glass
in the finding / that clear / in the
at last (clashing)

the
/ yours through that that is different energies dropping

coral leaves

invisible reaching

of same then bodies

sweet energies / fields
in the / delight
     where dreaming

or swimming / thru finding
or swimming / thru finding
or humming sounding
/ of dream-not-sleeping

with me there.

& you

over here.

in the finding / swimming / the through-ing
reaching

as before
play of that
humming or dream-seeing

/ thru of those bodies
of

while coral while
        (/ sleeping)

where you with me there.

& me with you here.

& at last
at last
at last
at last
waving!

invisible with-me coral
play of the clashing
                    thru

in here in the,
showing
(to me, where shall)

so

crshing & wving

the wth you waters / the how long waters / sometimes voices
/ coral that

or sounding saying

i th play the
of
wters

of field.
setting of grass
leaves waving of that whch

(would pour
/ show riches)

/ hum
make coral

after how long
upon you

island

that sometimes sounding
will make
and then
          clouds would

ready to

after how long

that long after long after long after long after how long
    swim

those here
that are
/ here.

(about mine)

& there
where
are your

/ at last
sweet.

        you can really
        have always
(been)

same bodies (waters) & coral

/ of still swum glass

The Author

Emily Critchley is the author of several poetry collections and editor of *Out of Everywhere 2: Linguistically Innovative Poetry by Women in North America & the UK* (Reality Street, 2016). This volume presents a new pamphlet-length collection, *Arrangements*, together with the sequence, *Movement Waving Not Sleeping*. Critchley has published critical articles on poetry, philosophy and feminism and is Senior Lecturer in English and Creative Writing at the University of Greenwich. She lives in London with her daughter.

Lightning Source UK Ltd.
Milton Keynes UK
UKHW041826131118
332284UK00001B/192/P